Wi
Shake

Rosie Dickins
Illustrated by Christa Unzner

Shakespeare consultant: Dr. Paul Edmondson,
Head of Learning, The Shakespeare Birthplace Trust

Reading consultant: Alison Kelly, Roehampton University

Series editor: Jane Chisholm
Designed by Michelle Lawrence and Natacha Goransky

First published in 2008 by Usborne Publishing Ltd.,
Usborne House, 83-85 Saffron Hill,
London EC1N 8RT, England.

www.usborne.com

Printed in India.

First published in America in 2008.

Contents

The Shakespeares' Home
Henley Street
Bridge Street
To London
Wood Street
High Street
Rother Street
Ely Street
Sheep Street
New Place
Scholar's Lane
Grammar School
Guild Hall and chapel
Church Street
Old Town
River Avon
Holy Trinity Church
N
W
E
S
Stratford-upon-Avon
around 1564

Chapter 1
Home in Stratford

Mr. Shakespeare was pacing nervously up and down his house in Stratford, unable to concentrate. His wife was about to have a baby and he hoped desperately that this new child would live longer than their two tiny daughters. They were already buried in the churchyard down by the river.

Suddenly, he heard a piercing wail...

Upstairs, his wife was smiling. She showed him a small, squirming bundle.

"It's a boy," she said. "Let's name him William."

"He's a fine, healthy baby," the midwife added.

Mr. Shakespeare sighed with relief, and went back to his work.

William's father was a skilful leather-worker. He knew how to shape and stitch soft kidskin to make elegant gloves. And he made extra money by selling wool – although he had to do it in secret, as he didn't have a wool-seller's permit. In fact, he was now so prosperous that he had even been asked to join the town council, leading to the job he liked best of all – drinking beer, as the town's official ale-taster.

This photograph shows the Shakespeare family home in Stratford, as it looks today. It is now open to the public.

As soon as William was old enough to ride, his father began to take him along when he went to buy wool and skins to make leather.

One day, on the way home for lunch, they overtook a small procession of carts and people in funny costumes.

"Wandering players!" exclaimed Mr. Shakespeare. "Heading for Stratford..."

William was thrilled. He had never been to a play before. "Can we go and see them?" he begged. "Please, please?" To his delight, his father was just as excited.

That afternoon, Mr. Shakespeare took William and his younger brother Gilbert to the town's Guild Hall, where plays were staged. He even bought them oranges – a rare treat in those days.

The hall was crowded with people on benches facing a rough wooden stage. Mr. Shakespeare and the boys sat at the front.

A trumpet sounded, silencing the hubbub. Then a grandly dressed actor appeared and made a magnificent speech about war. Next came a dastardly villain, accompanied by boos and hisses from the crowd.

After that, a couple of clowns ran around wildly, making everyone laugh. But William thought the best part was the ending. The play finished with a spectacular sword fight, which left most of the actors 'dead' in a heap.

William watched it all, agog. "Just wait till I tell the boys at school about this!" he thought.

William went to the town's junior school – although he was about to move up to Grammar School. The next day, as the class learned to write their names, he whispered the story of the play to his friends...

Shaxspere *Shakspere*

Shakespeare

"William, stop talking and sharpen your quill pen!" scolded his teacher. "You'll have to work harder at Grammar School. If you don't, they'll beat you with a birch rod!"

But not even the threat of beatings could stop William from day-dreaming about the players. Before long, he had made up his mind to be an actor too.

Unfortunately, as he soon discovered, Grammar School left no time for acting. There was too much hard work. Lessons started at six in the morning and didn't finish until five at night. There was even school on Saturdays and, on Sundays, they had to go to church with their families.

The boys (the school only took boys) had to learn ancient Greek and Latin, and study ancient Greek and Latin texts until they could recite them by heart. They studied ancient history, ancient plays and ancient rhetoric – the art of arguing and making speeches.

By the time he was 14, William knew a lot about ancient times. Then, one day, he came home to find his father looking worried.

"I'm afraid you're going to have to leave school and get a job," his father said sadly. "And I don't mean acting!" he added hastily, before William could open his mouth. "I mean a paying job. I'm having business trouble and we need the money."

"What did you have in mind?" asked William, trying not to look disappointed.

"Maybe, with all that schooling, you could work as a teacher?" said his father. "And I could use some help making gloves, too."

William sighed. "Still, at least I'll finally have some spare time," he thought to himself. "Maybe I could do some acting then. I could even write my own plays..."

Chapter 2
Anne

William's prospects suddenly looked a lot less bright. Over the next few years, things went from bad to worse.

Mr. Shakespeare was fined for charging too much interest on loans, and for selling wool illegally. Meanwhile, his family had grown. As well as William and Gilbert, there were three younger children to feed – Joan, Anne and Edmund. It was sometimes a struggle to make ends meet.

William still dreamed of acting. He longed to visit the big London playhouses. But for now he had to stay home and work.

Still, life in Stratford wasn't all drudgery. There was one thing that made William really cheerful. And her name was Anne.

Anne Hathaway lived in a cottage across the fields. William often went to see her with his troubles. She was sympathetic and pretty, and always made him feel better. One thing led to another and soon they were talking about marriage.

William was still only 18, and very young to get married – and not everyone thought Anne, at 26, was the right match for him.

The cottage where Anne Hathaway grew up, as it looks today

But William was in love. In fact, his feelings for Anne probably inspired one of his earliest love poems:

Those lips that Love's own hand did make...

So, one breezy November day, William and Anne were married in a little village church near Stratford.

Six months later, their first daughter, Susanna, was born. A couple of years later she was followed by twins, a boy and girl named Hamnet and Judith. William and Anne were delighted.

But, even with the children to occupy him, William was restless. He hadn't forgotten his dream of becoming an actor. He'd already begun writing some plays. He wasn't going to get anywhere in a country town like Stratford. But in London...

Home was getting a bit crowded, too. William and Anne were still living with William's family. And now his brother Gilbert was old enough to work, they didn't need William's help so much any more.

So the next time a group of players came to Stratford, William seized his chance. He went to see them, nervously clutching a bundle of his writings. They were on their way to London – and when they had read his ideas for plays, they invited him to join them.

William was thrilled. Now he just had to break the news to his family. "The players have asked me to go to London with them," he announced later, over dinner. "At last I can go and try my luck as an actor!"

"I want to be an actor too," said Edmund, his little brother, who always copied him.

"You need to grow up first, Ed!"

Anne frowned. "It's at least a hundred miles to London," she pointed out. "That's much too far for the children and me."

"You'll have to stay here," William agreed. "But I'll come back and visit as often as I can. I'm sure I can get some writing work in London. And if all goes well, I'll soon be a famous actor!"

Chapter 3
London

A few years later, William was well settled in London. It was a dirty, noisy, bustling place. People packed the cobbled streets, pushing to avoid the stinking gutters. All day long, traders yelled, hooves clopped and cartwheels clattered.

But William loved it. From his lodgings, it was just a short walk to the city's best playhouses – The Theatre, The Curtain and newest of all, The Rose. Here, huge crowds gathered each afternoon to see the latest plays.

William had begun to make a name for himself, too. But not everything had gone according to plan. He had done a bit of acting, it was true. But it was his writing that was really in demand. The big playhouses changed their shows almost every day, so they needed lots of material. William soon found himself working on scripts.

At first, the other playwrights had sneered at him because he hadn't gone to a university, as they had. But that hadn't stopped him from creating some of the most popular characters. Now, the others were getting jealous and calling him "upstart crow" and other names.

William was too busy to care. Today, his new play about King Henry VI was opening at The Rose. He hurried to the playhouse straight after breakfast. It was across the river in Southwark – a seedy area full of gaming houses, fighting pits and drinking dens. The wooden walls of The Rose towered above them all, its flag fluttering in the breeze.

This old engraving shows London in Shakespeare's time, looking across the river to the north. Below, you can see two round buildings – The Rose, and a bear-fighting pit called The Beargarden.

At London Bridge, William paused to admire the boats – graceful sailing ships, narrow barges and bobbing rowboats ferrying people back and forth. The bridge ended at a large stone gatehouse. Above the gate, a row of gruesome, grinning heads were stuck up on spikes – the punishment for traitors. William shivered and walked on quickly.

The engraving shows London Bridge crowded with shops and houses. At the time, it was the only bridge in the city, and the fortified gatehouse at the end was closed at night.

When William arrived, he found his friend Richard Burbage already struggling into his costume; he was playing the King, and William, one of the lords.

The actors spent the morning rehearsing, with William making sure they got their lines right. They went over the sword fights, and the actors who were going to be stabbed hid bags of pigs' blood under their shirts. The boy playing Henry's queen combed his wig. Women weren't allowed to perform in public, so their parts went to boys with smooth chins and high voices.

Eventually, the audience began to file in. "Groundlings" paid a penny to stand in the yard, at the mercy of the weather, while the wealthy paid tuppence for the luxury of a seat in one of the covered galleries. A few pennies more bought you a seat in an exclusive balcony right above the action.

Soon, the place was filled with a chattering, nut-munching, expectant crowd. It was time to start.

"I hope they like it," William thought nervously.

He needn't have worried. From the first trumpet call to the final battle, the play was a triumph. The crowd oohed and aahed in all the right places, and even cried at the heroic death of one brave English soldier.

The play was repeated many times over the coming months, attracting an audience of thousands. William had written a smash hit. A great career beckoned. He bought himself a stylish new fitted jacket, or doublet, and a stack of paper and quills, and set to work on his next script.

But then, disaster struck. The first William knew of it was a red cross painted on the door of a house a few streets away. It was followed by another, and another...

When William asked his landlord what they meant, the old man frowned. "Death," he said grimly. "Those crosses – they mark houses with the plague."

In London's crowded, filthy streets, it was all too easy for disease to spread – and no disease was deadlier than the plague. Its victims dropped dead in days.

When someone in a house became sick, a cross was painted on the door to warn others to stay away. Many Londoners fled the city in terror, hoping to escape infection.

This old engraving – titled "Lord, have mercy on London" – shows a skeleton dancing on the coffins of plague victims.

As a precaution, all the playhouses were shut. No plays meant no money. But William and his fellow actors still had to earn a living – especially William, with children to support. They sat glumly around the empty playhouse, trying to think of a plan.

"We could pawn our clothes," suggested John Hemmings, fingering a velvet cloak.

"And then stay at home with nothing to wear!" laughed Will Kemp.

"William, have you tried writing to the Earl of Southampton?" Richard broke in. "He's very rich and he likes your writing – he might help you out."

Richard was right. The Earl sent the young author money and offered to become his patron. At last, William could stop worrying. It was a huge relief.

To show his admiration for the Earl, William wrote a long poem about Venus, the Roman goddess of love, and dedicated it to him. The poem was witty and daring, just the sort of thing a dashing young Earl might enjoy. When it was finished, William took it to a printing shop near Saint Paul's Cathedral.

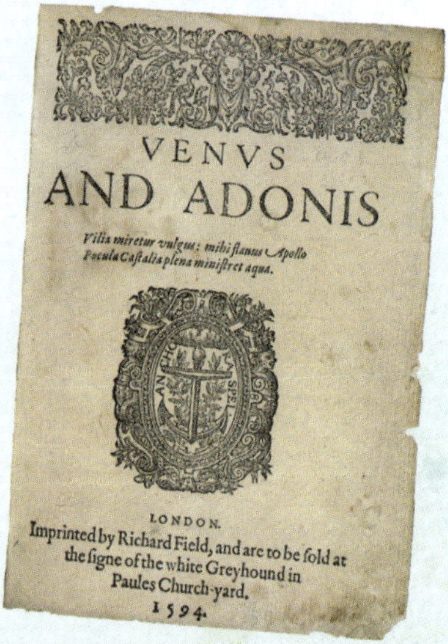
VENVS
AND ADONIS

Vilia miretur vulgus: mihi flauus Apollo
Pocula Castalia plena ministret aqua.

LONDON.
Imprinted by Richard Field, and are to be sold at
the signe of the white Greyhound in
Paules Church-yard.
1594.

This is the title page of the poem as it first appeared in print.

William had never published anything before, but the poem was a huge success. The first batch of printed copies sold out so fast, the shop had to print a second batch... and a third...

Delighted, William quickly set to work on another long poem, this time a tragedy, again dedicated to the Earl. He also began composing a series of sonnets – elegant love poems, all exactly 14 lines long.

Shall I compare thee to a summer's day?
Thou art more lovely and more temperate.
Rough winds do shake the darling buds of May,
And summer's lease hath all too short a date...

Meanwhile, the playhouses remained firmly shut. William's hopes of glory on the stage were beginning to seem like a distant dream.

Chapter 4
Fame and fortune

The playhouses stayed closed for a year and a half while the plague raged. Each night, carts rolled slowly down the streets to collect the dead. There were so many bodies, they had to be buried in huge pits. It was a terrible time; but gradually the disease passed and life began to get back to normal.

One evening, William was sitting in a tavern with Richard when their friend Will Kemp burst in, looking very excited.

"They're going to reopen the playhouses," he announced.

"We've got to get ready..."

"But who will employ us? All the acting companies have gone," Richard pointed out.

"Why don't we form our own company?" said William. "After all, Richard, you're the best tragic actor in London – and Will, you're the best comedian. And I've got some wonderful ideas for plays."

"Yes – and if we're lucky, we might even find a rich patron," Richard added. "It always helps to have connections!"

"It's a great plan. Let's have some ale to celebrate!" Will exclaimed.

To their delight, their plans caught the eye of the Lord Chamberlain, who was in charge of arranging entertainment for the Queen. He offered to be the patron of their new company, so they became known as the Lord Chamberlain's Men. But, even with his help, setting everything up was hard work.

Richard and Will hired more actors and rented a room at an inn known as The Cross Keys. William scribbled away furiously at the scripts. Then they needed costumes, and rehearsals, and someone to sell tickets...

Eventually, they were ready to open with two plays about English kings, Richard II and Henry IV. Both drew big audiences. William's writing was just as clever as before. Richard made a memorable monarch; his heroic speeches thrilled the crowds.

But Will Kemp stole the show as a knight named Falstaff, a plump, cheerful rogue. The audience loved him, and he loved making them laugh. He kept inventing extra jokes, to the annoyance of the other actors.

In spite of their success, something was troubling William. Every play they did had to be licensed by the Queen's censor. The censor would not allow anything that criticized the Queen, even indirectly, so any play about royalty was a sensitive matter. "I've seen what happens to traitors," William thought, remembering the heads on London Bridge. "Perhaps it's time for a new subject."

So William set to work again, this time on a tragic love story entitled *Romeo and Juliet*. It told the tale of a young couple who fall in love against the wishes of their families – and it was another smash hit.

The actors gave magnificent performances, especially Richard as Romeo. And audiences adored the play's romantic atmosphere, full of flamboyant speeches and flaming passions.

A few months later, William followed it with another play about love, this time a light-hearted comedy. *A Midsummer Night's Dream* is a magical story about mismatched lovers and mischievous fairies, where everyone lives happily ever after – even though the Fairy Queen falls in love with a man with a donkey's head.

William's quill seemed to be magic, too. People flocked to see everything he wrote, and paid good money to do so. In summer, the company performed to huge audiences in the big, open-air playhouses.

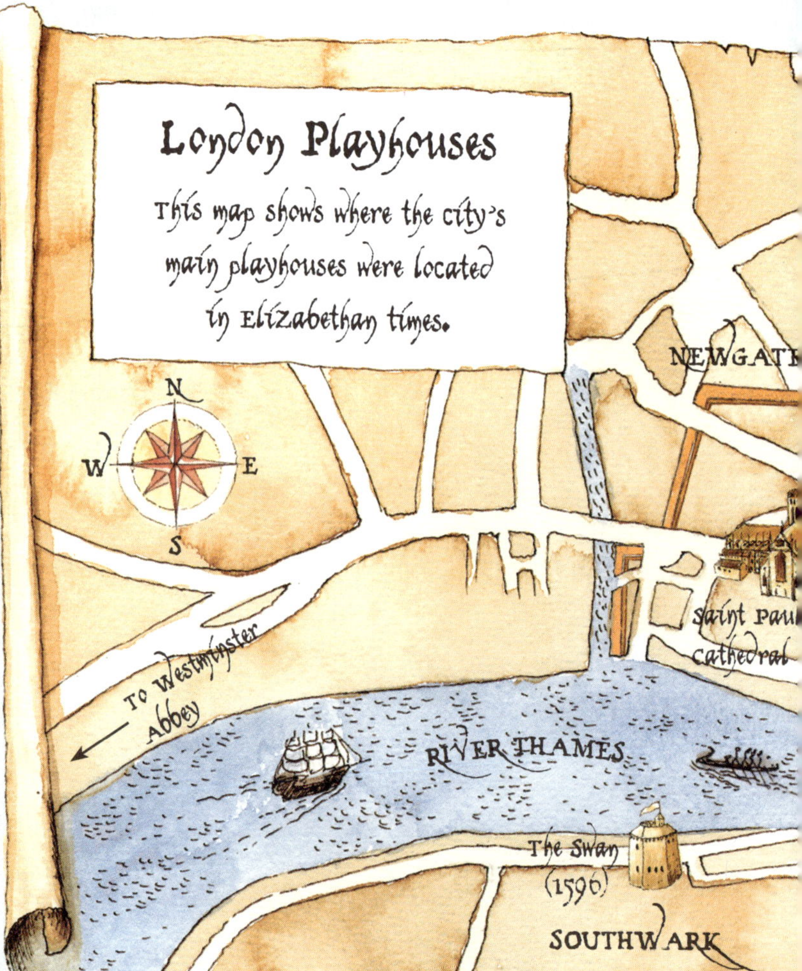

Mostly they played at The Theatre, which was run by Richard's family. In the winter, they moved to The Cross Keys Inn, which was smaller but more comfy. Here, at least, they had the choice of playing indoors, with a roof over their heads, or out in the yard.

It wasn't all smooth sailing, of course. They had many rivals. The Admiral's Men were pulling in the crowds too, and often performed for the Queen. Then there was a craze for children's companies, where all the actors were young boys.

And success brought its own problems. People complained about the crowds and the noise caused by popular plays, and a strict religious group known as the Puritans claimed all plays were immoral. Some protesters even called for the playhouses to be closed down. Luckily for William and his friends, the Queen enjoyed plays too much herself to agree.

But if William was ever troubled by any of this, far worse was in store...

Chapter 5

Troubled times

The year 1596 was a terrible one in the English countryside. Months of appalling weather made the crops fail, so people began to starve. Weakened by lack of food, many became ill. In some places, including Stratford, there were riots as people's despair turned to violence. William sent his family money for food, but times were hard for everyone.

In August, William and Anne's son Hamnet fell ill. Anne wrote to tell her husband it was serious, but her letter took days to reach him. Before it arrived, Hamnet was dead. He was just 11 years old.

William and Anne had lost their only son. They were devastated.

In his sorrow, William threw himself into his work, including a new play called *King John*. He was trying to keep himself from thinking about his loss, but his feelings sometimes showed through his writing.

Grief fills the room up of my absent child...

Oh Lord! My boy... my fair son!

Now, William's thoughts turned more and more to his family. It was too late to help Hamnet, but he bought the second biggest house in Stratford, an elegant brick building called New Place, for Anne and the girls, hoping to spend more time there with them.

William also promised to help his younger brother Edmund, who still wanted to become an actor, to find a job in London. And for his father, who had always longed to have his own coat of arms, he went to see the herald at the College of Arms in London. A few weeks later, Mr. Shakespeare proudly unrolled an official scroll.

It was a certificate showing his new coat of arms, a golden shield with a drawing of a spear, and a motto in Latin: *Non Sanz Droict,* meaning *Not Without Right.*

William's sadness didn't stop him from writing hit plays. But they began to reveal a darker side. In his next comedy, *The Merchant of Venice*, the hero is pursued by a moneylender demanding a pound of his flesh as payment for a debt.

He also wrote a sequel to his earlier hit about Henry IV, describing how the crown passes to the King's son – who then has to banish his roguish old friend, Falstaff.

That might have been the end of Falstaff but his character, played with enthusiasm by Will Kemp, was just too popular. So William brought him back for their next play, *The Merry Wives of Windsor*, a comic romp about Falstaff in love. It was such a success, the actors even claimed to have performed it for Queen Elizabeth.

This portrait shows Queen Elizabeth at the height of her reign.

But while the Queen enjoyed plays, she would not tolerate any hint of rebellion. When an unlicensed play about her government opened at The Swan playhouse, the authorities reacted swiftly and severely. They closed the playhouse, confiscated the scripts and threw three of the actors involved into jail. Then, to the horror of every actor in London, the Queen banned all plays in the city for that summer.

"Summer is our busiest time," said Richard despairingly when he heard the news. "We can only play the big open-air venues in good weather."

"She must be worried," mused William. "Maybe she thinks we'll start a riot..."

"But if we can't act, we'll soon be stone broke and starving!" wailed Will Kemp. "What are we going to do?"

"There's no choice – we'll have to go on tour," Richard decided.

So they and the rest of the company packed their bags.

It was a bad time to be touring. After the famine, few people outside London had money to spend on plays. But the actors did what they could, playing to small crowds at country inns and begging invitations from the local gentry.

As soon as they dared, they hurried back to London. To their relief, they found Queen Elizabeth was glad to have them back again.

"The Queen has asked us to play at court three times this Christmas," William wrote happily to Anne. "The Admiral's Men have only been asked once!" he added, gloating. "But there's a problem with our playhouse..."

The lease on The Theatre had expired, so the Lord Chamberlain's Men had been forced to move to The Curtain. It wasn't a bad place, but it was much smaller – and they were attracting bigger and bigger crowds. They needed more room.

Richard and his brother pleaded with the landlord to renew the lease. In the meantime, the players crammed as many visitors as they could into The Curtain.

Every afternoon, the little yard was packed with people cheering the hero of William's latest drama, or doubled up laughing at his new comedy, *Much Ado About Nothing*.

The landlord refused to budge. A year later, they were still at The Curtain.

"It's ridiculous," Richard fumed, as they turned away crowds yet again. "My family owns that playhouse!"

"What do you mean?" asked William.

"The lease was just for the land. My family owns the buildings," explained Richard. "Not that they're much use where they are," he added ruefully.

"I think we can do something about that, lads," Will put in, grinning. "Why don't we just move the playhouse?" It was crazy – but no one had a better idea.

One crisp, frosty morning soon after Christmas, the company stole into The Theatre carrying saws, crowbars and hammers. It didn't take long to dismantle the old playhouse. Then they carried the timbers across the river to Southwark and began putting them together on a new site.

When the landlord found out, he was furious, but there was nothing he could do.

By the start of the summer season, the new playhouse was finished. It had round, whitewashed walls, three levels of galleries and a broad stage jutting out into an enormous yard.

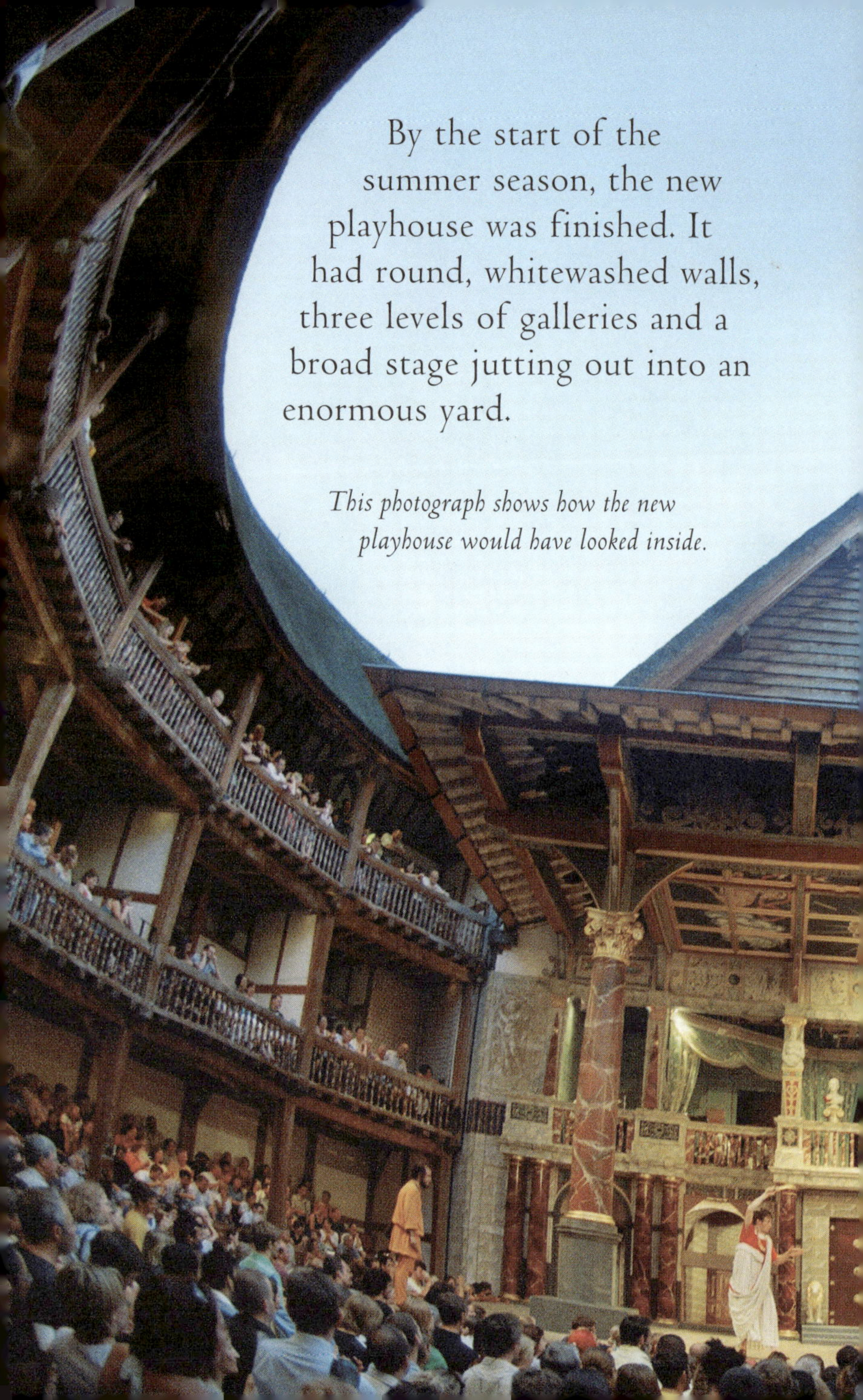

This photograph shows how the new playhouse would have looked inside.

Above the stage, there was a canopy decorated with a golden sun and stars, supported by two marble-painted columns.

"It's like a whole world in here," said Richard, looking around proudly. "Let's call it The Globe."

The photograph was taken inside the replica Globe which stands in Southwark today.

The company's problems should have been over. But you wouldn't have known it from listening to Will and William. They were constantly bickering over Will's habit of making up new lines.

"You've got to stop it, Will," William snapped one day. "You keep dancing around and making stupid jokes, and it's spoiling my script."

"If you don't like it, I can go and dance somewhere else!" retorted Will. "I'll dance a jig all the way to..." (he paused to think of a town) "...Norwich, you'll see!"

With that, he stormed off, leaving the company without its star comedian.

To replace him, Richard hired a new actor named Robert Armin. He was a thin, clever fellow, nothing like Will, but very funny in his own way. And, to William's relief, he stuck to the script.

Apart from losing Will, who really was stubbornly dancing his way to Norwich, things were going wonderfully.

Delighted with their new playhouse, William dashed off hit after hit – from the sassy romantic comedy *As You Like It* to the Roman tragedy *Julius Caesar*. But his greatest triumph was a play about a troubled young Danish Prince named Hamlet.

It seemed the Lord Chamberlain's Men were the hottest tickets in town. The only question was what to do next.

Chapter 6

The King's Men

As Queen Elizabeth grew older, her health began to fail. Before long, everyone was gossiping about who would rule England after her. The Earl of Essex, who had fallen out with the Queen, saw a chance to get his revenge.

"If I led an uprising, I could take the crown myself," he reasoned. "Elizabeth has no children, so there would be no one to oppose me. I just need a way to start things off."

Essex decided that he needed an angry mob, and that a good way to get one would be to stage a stirring play. So he sent for William. "You know that play of yours where rebels topple the King," he began.

"You mean that scene in *Richard II*?" William asked. "The censor told us to leave it out. He said it might cause trouble."

"Exactly!" thought Essex. Aloud, he said: "Of course for a special performance, I'll pay you twice what you normally get."

William couldn't resist such an offer. On the appointed afternoon, the Globe audience watched King Richard lose his crown. But at the end, instead of starting a revolution, everyone went home.

The next day, when Essex marched into the streets, he found only the Queen's spies waiting to arrest him. He was tried and sentenced to death. Then the Lord Chamberlain's Men were summoned to explain why they had staged the banned play.

"It was just for money," they pleaded.

The Queen frowned. "I pardon you," she said eventually. "However, you will perform for me on the night before Essex's execution, so you do not forget what happens to traitors."

Although the old Queen had survived Essex's plot, she couldn't live forever. A couple of years later she died, leaving the crown to her cousin, James.

The new King was a big fan of William's plays. He summoned the Lord Chamberlain's Men to the palace almost immediately.

King James, dressed in fur-trimmed velvet for his coronation

"I want you to rename your company," he told them grandly. "You're the King's Men now – oh, and I'd like you to come to my coronation, too."

The coronation ceremony took place at Westminster Abbey. It was a sumptuous affair. To make sure the players were well-dressed for the occasion, the King gave each of them a length of fine scarlet cloth to make a new doublet.

That Christmas, the King's Men staged three different comedies at Hampton Court Palace. The King was delighted with his new company.

"Well done Shakespeare, old chap," he muttered after a performance of *Measure for Measure*. "Jolly good show! I liked that crafty Duke character. It's just a shame there were no witches."

King James was obsessed with witches. He had taken part in witch trials and had written a book called *Daemonologie*, all about witches and how to spot them.

So, to please him, William made sure one of his next plays, *Macbeth*, contained three spell-casting crones.

But there was something else on William's mind – family. Just before *Macbeth*, he had been writing a tragedy about a King and his daughters, entitled *King Lear*. Now he began a comedy, *The Winter's Tale*, about a lost daughter.

"How I miss my own daughters!" he thought to himself, watching the girl's joyful reunion with her parents at the end of the play. "Maybe it's time to go home..."

Chapter 7

Back to Stratford

William was missing Stratford more and more. After so many years, the excitement of London life had worn off. He visited his family as often as he could, but it wasn't enough. "I want to be there when our daughters get married," he wrote to Anne, "and I want to spend more time with you."

In the meantime, however, the King's Men needed a new play. He couldn't leave London just yet.

For their next show, William created a magical romance called *The Tempest*, set on an island haunted by strange spirits. There, in exile, live an old magician named Prospero and his daughter, Miranda.

Prospero uses his magic to shipwreck a young prince, who immediately falls in love with Miranda. Then, as a happy ending approaches, Prospero renounces magic and promises that he will destroy his magic staff and spellbook.

Everyone was delighted with the new play except Richard, who knew what that speech meant. "Prospero's farewell to magic... that's your farewell to writing, isn't it?" he asked.

"Yes – it's time to retire," William replied quietly. "I'm getting old."

"But we need you!" Richard pleaded. "No one else can write like you."

The other actors joined in. No one wanted William to go. In the end, he agreed to work on three more plays with a young writer named John Fletcher – including a new drama about King Henry VIII, to be staged at The Globe.

"It'll be wonderful," Richard said excitedly. "No expense will be spared. We'll get grand embroidered costumes for the courtiers. And we'll fire real cannons to mark the entrance of the King."

Unfortunately, as it turned out, the cannons were a disastrous idea. The Globe was built of wood, and the galleries were thatched with straw. In dry weather, it was like a pile of kindling waiting for a flame.

During a performance at the end of June, one cannon shot went astray, showering the roof with sparks. While everyone concentrated on the drama unfolding on stage, a tiny orange light began to flicker in the straw. Within minutes, huge flames were billowing across the thatch and licking down the walls.

The fire spread so fast, there was nothing anyone could do. The players watched helplessly as the flames devoured everything. One man's breeches even caught fire and had to be put out with beer. In less than an hour, The Globe was a smoking ruin.

"Well, at least no one was hurt," said Richard. "And we can soon rebuild..."

William interrupted his old friend. "I'm too old to start all over again," he said. "This is it, Rich – I'm going home."

This time, nobody could change William's mind. As soon as he had packed his bags and found himself a horse, he set out on the long ride back to Stratford.

When his tired horse finally clopped up the road to New Place, Anne and the girls rushed out to greet him. Soon he was sitting in the kitchen, laughing as they fussed over him. Judith brought him a mug of ale while Anne put away his things. And Susanna, who had married a local doctor, proudly introduced him to his new granddaughter, Elizabeth.

"It's good to be home!" he sighed.

Sadly, it was not to be a long retirement. Just three years later, William became ill.

"Fetch a lawyer," he told his wife as he lay in bed with fever. "I want to make my will. I'm leaving you the second-best bed – our marriage bed – to remember me by! The best guest bed can go to Susanna. And Judith can have my big silver bowl."

The lawyer came just in time. Not long afterwards, William was dead.

He was buried one rainy April day in his local church, where Anne had a monument erected to his memory. It was a statue of her husband with an inscription comparing him to the great writers of ancient Greek and Roman times, and it is still there today.

As a further tribute, William's friends published the first collection of his plays – known as the First Folio – ensuring his name would live on as one of the most celebrated playwrights of all time.

Shakespeare's life

Around April 23rd, 1564 – I am born in Stratford-upon-Avon.

1582 – I marry Anne Hathaway.

1583 – Our daughter Susanna is born.

1585 – The twins, Hamnet and Judith, are born.

About 1587 – I go to London to try my luck as an actor, but find more success as a writer.

1592 – The plague hits London; thousands die and the playhouses are forced to close.

1594 – The playhouses reopen. Richard Burbage, Will Kemp and I form our company, the Lord Chamberlain's Men.

1596 – My dear son Hamnet dies.

1599 – We open our own playhouse, The Globe.

1601 – The Earl of Essex tries to use one of my plays in a plot against the Queen. I have a narrow escape.

1603 – Queen Elizabeth dies. Her successor, King James, makes our company the King's Men.

1613 – The Globe burns down. I go back to live in Stratford.

April 23rd, 1616 – *After a short illness, William dies.*

1623 – *William's friends publish his plays.*

P.S. Did you wonder exactly what William did after he left school, and how he got to London? Like many things that happened so long ago, there is no way to be sure. He may have helped his father with the family business, but some people think he became a schoolteacher or joined a band of players. According to one account, he was caught poaching deer and ran away. There are lots of stories, but little evidence to support any of them – so you'll have to decide what you think for yourself.

Shakespeare's works

William wrote at least 40 plays and over 150 poems – this page lists the most famous. He didn't record exactly when he wrote them, but experts have worked out rough dates based on historical references.

1589-92	King Henry VI (Parts 1, 2 and 3)
1593	Venus and Adonis
1595-96	King Richard II, Romeo and Juliet, A Midsummer Night's Dream
1596-97	King John, The Merchant of Venice
1597-98	King Henry IV (Parts 1 and 2)
1598-99	Much Ado About Nothing, Henry V, The Merry Wives of Windsor
1599-1600	Julius Caesar, As You Like It
1600-01	Hamlet
1602-03	Othello
1603-04	Measure for Measure
1604-05	King Lear
1605-06	Macbeth
Before 1609	The Sonnets
1610-11	The Winter's Tale
1611-12	The Tempest
1612-13	King Henry VIII*

*co-written with John Fletcher

This photograph shows Anne's memorial to William, which still hangs above his grave in Stratford. The quill in his hand is changed in a special ceremony every year. The town also holds big celebrations on his birthday.

Index

Internet links

You can find out more about William Shakespeare, listen to speeches from his plays or explore inside The Globe by going to the Usborne Quicklinks Website at **www.usborne-quicklinks.com** and typing in the keywords 'yr shakespeare'.

Please note that Usborne Publishing cannot be responsible for the content of any website other than its own.

Acknowledgements

Cover: Shakespeare portrait © Royal Shakespeare Company; View of London © The British Library. **Title page:** Shakespeare portrait © Bettmann/Corbis. **Page 6:** Shakespeare family home © Paul Thompson/Corbis. **Page 14:** Anne Hathaway's cottage © Ellen Rooney/Getty Images. **Pages 20-21:** View of London © The British Library. **Page 25:** Plague woodcut © Private Collection/Bridgeman Art Library. **Page 26:** Venus and Adonis © The British Library. **Page 40:** Queen Elizabeth I © Visual Arts Library (London)/Alamy. **Pages 46-47** Shakespeare's Globe interior © John Tramper (photo)/Shakespeare's Globe Picture Library. **Page 52:** King James I © Mary Evans Picture Library. **Page 63:** Shakespeare memorial © Bridgeman Art Library.